MINDFULNESS 101

CONCEPTS, MISCONCEPTIONS & PRACTICES

Zoey Matthews

NEW YORK, NY

Zoey Matthews

Book Layout ©2017 Book Design Templates

Ordering Information:
Quantity sales. Special discounts are available on quantity purchases by corporations, associations, and others. For details, contact the Author

Mindfulness 101-Concepts, Misconceptions & Practices/Zoey Matthews. —1st ed.
ISBN 978-1545256237

Contents

Introduction 1

Who You Are 3

What Mindfulness is Not 7

Where You Want to Be 11

Mental Clarity/ Well-Being 13

Better Physical Health 17

Better Emotional Health... 21

What Exactly is Mindfulness? 25

    Acceptance... 26

    Practice 29

Preparing For Mindfulness 31

    The Planning... 31

    Being Present 32

    Staying Present.. 34

Getting Started 39

Steps to Mindful Meditation.................................... 43

The Importance of the Breath and Mindfulness 47

Mindfulness for Busy People 53

What is Holding You Back? 57

Conclusion 63

About the Author 65

"There are only two ways to live your life. One is as though nothing is a miracle. The other is as though everything is a miracle."

—— ALBERT EINSTEIN

CHAPTER 1

Introduction

The mind is an intricate organ that manages thousands of tasks at any given moment. It is easy to rush through life without paying attention to it. Mindfulness is the tool you can use to bring yourself back to awareness. Not only is it a fantastic way to improve your physical health, it can positively affect your emotional and mental health. Here is the story of mindfulness and what it can do for you!

CHAPTER 2

Who You Are

L et's look at your life now. You are likely busy from morning to night. Most people get up at the crack of dawn, get their kids ready, let the pets out, get everyone fed, organize themselves, get everyone where they must go and then get to work. This, of course, is all within the first few hours of being awake.

After that, you're off to your own job, where your boss barks orders, your co-workers want to talk and get your input about their projects, your customers want your time, you have emails to respond to, emails to send...the list goes on and on. After THAT, you must do everything again, but in reverse...pick up the kids, get them home, help them with their homework, get dinner on the table, clean up, put the children to bed and possibly have a few minutes to yourself before you go to bed, only to start the process again the next morning. Does this sound familiar?

Often, we find ourselves in this never-ending cycle of activities. It is a day that repeats itself over and over again, leaving no time for what we want—or need—to do. Maybe you're a professional who is just overwhelmed with life. Maybe you're a parent who is caring for small children. Maybe you're caring for an aging parent. Or maybe you're just a single adult trying to get through life!

Regardless of what your life is like, you probably don't have time throughout the day for yourself. Did you know that ABC News conducted a study to find out how many people are overwhelmed with their lives? Of the 1,000 people surveyed, more than one-fourth stated that they were completely overwhelmed with their lives. More than 200 stated that they worked between six and seven days a week. One-fourth stated that they, in general, didn't use their vacation time.

Regardless of the amount of overwhelm they felt, respondents stated that they were most prone to neglecting themselves and their needs and felt less success with personal relationships. They were more focused on achievements in the eyes of others (think bosses, spouses, children, parents, etc.) and by choice neglected themselves and their own needs.

Here's another major study. According to NPR, the Harvard School of Public Health found that 25 percent of all Americans believe they experienced a great deal of stress in the past month. Half of adults say they have gone through intense stress within the past year. That adds up to approximately 115 million people. Study leaders said that that is likely a tragic understatement because many people are stressed but completely unaware of it.

Eldar Sharif, a psychologist at Princeton University, said that the mind is like bandwidth. Yes, it can handle a variety of inputs at one time, but there is a limit. He added that some things get neglected, or at a minimum slowed down, by the limitation. Over time, stress can become a chronic issue that compromises health, financial stability and relationships. The bottom line is that people today have worked themselves into a schedule frenzy. They are obviously intensely responsible, which in itself is a great thing, but when you look at the price they pay, is it worth it?

Stress is a constant in people's lives today, and the core of it is not negotiable. Consider Melinda James of Tallahassee, Florida. She is a 39-year-old mother of three young children. She began her career as a retail worker but decided to make a better life for herself and her family by enrolling in an online college. Her goal? To become a teacher. Though she made it through the program with flying colors, because of the recession of 2008 she never found that job for which she had prepared so hard. She's in arrears on her loans, which means her transcripts are unavailable—making it impossible to prove to potential employers that she has a degree.

Then there is Colin McGinness. He works at a local restaurant as an assistant manager. He has sole custody of two children under the age of eight and worries about them. He has very limited days off at work, so when one of his children needs him, he must take the pay cut. He confirms that sometimes he must take more time off than he spends on the job. He also said that the responsibilities of being a working man and a single father are sometimes "too much." In fact, his life has gotten to the point where he has repeated panic attacks over relatively small details. Recently, he experienced shortness of breath and was brought to tears because he forgot the baked goods his daughter needed to bring to school for a bake sale.

The human condition is made to manage stress. Since the early days of civilization, people have had responsibilities, including daily tasks for individual survival, tasks for their tribe's survival and for their offspring. Activities were much more harrowing than what they are today, with people having to find ways to hunt, forage and sustain themselves. Though those days were more difficult physically, the evolution mentally has changed, adding strains to the everyday world. What has changed throughout the centuries is the tools available to take care of survival, tasks and offspring. The tools encourage even more mental efficiency. Efficiency means that the demand for performance is that much higher. Just think about the office setting 50 years ago—typewriters and a typist could output only one document at a time. When carbon copy paper was created, it was considered a miracle—two sheets at once? Now, with the advancement of technology, thousands of copies of a document can be created within minutes. Or consider the cars of the early 1920s, which could blast down the roads at a whopping 45 to 50 miles per hour max. Imagine having a new vehicle these days that hit only that speed. You'd likely take back your car within minutes!

So, what is the answer for Americans who are stressed? What is the answer for those who aren't even aware of how stressed they are? The problem with stress is that it is a known precipitator of mental problems, poor physical health and struggling emotional health. Just ask anyone who has dealt with a lot of stress for any length of time. They will tell you about the toll it has taken on their bodies—physically and beyond.

The author of "Take the Stress Out of Your Life" Jay Winner said, "Stress doesn't only make us feel awful emotionally...[but] it can also exacerbate just about any health condition you can think of." Recent studies have shown that stress is directly linked to and a cause of increased heart disease, depression, diabetes, asthma, gastrointestinal issues and obesity. You know when you hear about the classic "Type A" personality? Research proves that these people, in general, have higher rates of heart problems and high blood pressure from the start. Add a stressful life to that and you have a recipe for disaster.

All around are signs that stress is reaching new heights. Whether you are a busy single parent of one managing a sales job or a middle-ager juggling a household with a family of five, you are a target for stress and all the negatives that come along with it. The bottom line is that everyone is stressed and eliminating stress is virtually impossible in today's world. The only thing to do is look at your life and find ways to manage that stress. Finding tools that you can use in a pinch and work on long-term is critical to making your life as manageable as possible.

The good news is that those tools are available—to everyone. They don't always come easily, though. As much as people claim to want to get rid of stress, the reality is that they are accustomed to it. Letting go of it is hard. What you can do, though, is seek the solutions that will help you be more mindful of the now. Find the tools that work for you and that will allow you to set your mile-a-minute thinking on pause. When you do learn how to put the tools to work for you, you will be able to see the benefits of:

A calmer general disposition
Better immune function
A more relaxed demeanor
Better sleep
Better digestion
More energy
Fewer physical ailments
A more positive focus

Welcome to the journey toward finding out what mindfulness is and how you can use it for your life. Yes, it is a journey and not the kind that will end in a few days or even weeks. However, the promise is that if you continue to focus and apply the techniques of mindfulness, you will find it to be one of the best decisions you have ever made!

CHAPTER 3

What Mindfulness is Not

Y ou may have heard the term "mindfulness" thrown around. There is a lot of misinformation out there, with protracted definitions of the word, but we will look at what it really means. First, let's cover what it is NOT. Here are 10 mistaken ideas about mindfulness that are relatively common in today's world:

> *"I need perfect quiet to be mindful, and that isn't going to happen."*

It would be nice to have complete quiet time throughout the day to focus on being mindful; however, it just isn't the case for 99 percent of people. Lives don't lend themselves well to the word "perfect" very often. If you're waiting for that "perfect quiet" to get yourself going on, you'll be waiting a long time. It's just like waiting for the "perfect time" to get married, to have kids, to start a new diet, to start saving for retirement, etc. Wait too long and your time may be out! If you're ready to put in the work, though, you'll see the benefits that millions of others do.

> *"People use mindfulness meditations to escape their reality rather than face it."*

Mindfulness is not a form of organized denial. In fact, without committing to the truth and seeing it as it is, you will be unable to find the focus you need for mindfulness. The first part is to be honest—about everything. In addition, when you decide to work on mindfulness, you'll understand your issues, sort them out and bring real-life, proactive solutions to the table. The goal is to help you solve your problems...or at a minimum, to give you the tools to manage them in the best way possible.

"Mindfulness is about being self-centered and self-absorbed."

Yes, it is self-centered, but self-absorption is not synonymous with that. In fact, taking time out of your schedule to focus on your needs will make you better for those around you. You can't keep stretching yourself so thinly that you lack effectiveness, and that's what studies show people do. Recall the above statement about "bandwidth"? Spread it to too many users and it gets slow and lags. The same thing happens when we don't find ways to stop and take care of our own mental health.

"Mindfulness takes a long time to understand and benefit you."

It can benefit a person immediately, but in general, no, mindfulness is not always an overnight success for its studiers. It can take time to find out what works for you, for your schedule and for your habits. The value, though, is that once you do find the perfect fit, you'll know it. You will see results in your life, including diminished stress, better physical health and more healthy emotions. If you knew that a daily or weekly practice could help your entire body in the long run, wouldn't you at least be excited about testing it out?

"Mindfulness is great if you're religious; if you're not, why bother?"

The religious aspect is inconsequential. Some of the most religious people never take the time to be mindful. Some of the least religious people are the most mindful. The two are not mutually inclusive or exclusive. The two can each stand on their own. What you should know is that whether you address mindfulness in a religious or non-religious way, you will see an overall benefit to your life. It may even open the door to religion if that is what you're seeking.

"All meditation is the same."

Over the years, mindfulness meditation techniques have undergone much development. Ancient civilizations understood the power of focusing on the mind and its attention. Because meditation has been around for centuries, you can benefit from its many forms. If one method doesn't work for you, there are plenty of others to try. There are enough that you'll likely find the perfect fit. The key is to be open and willing to try as many options as possible until you find the ideal one for your life.

"Mindfulness has little practical value."

This isn't a purely spiritual pursuit. Remember that the human body is made up of three parts: physical, spiritual and emotional. All three are closely tied and you can't improve one without benefitting the others. Any time you can slow yourself down and get centered, you'll find benefit on all levels. Those benefits can easily expand and flow outward to the rest of your life. If anything, the people around you will see the difference and ask you what you're on to!

"It takes too much time to practice mindfulness."

Yes, some people have the luxury of partaking in hours of daily meditation. They can center themselves with little to no distraction and can easily reap the benefits. Is that the norm? Nope! Still, there are millions of people with busy lives who manage to fit mindfulness into their worlds. Does it take determination? Yes. Does it take a schedule? Yes. Does it take discipline? Yes. Is it worth it? In the end—unequivocally, yes! Just ask the millions of people who already delved into it and are reaping the benefits daily. They will tell you about how it can be the life-changing activity they need to be more productive and balanced people.

"Mindfulness is too difficult."

Many people try mindfulness and, without immediate success, give up, claiming it is "too difficult" or "too much wasted energy." The truth is that in today's world people are used to immediate results. If they want something, all they have to do is click a few buttons on the keyboard and they find it. They can literally have it delivered to their front doors within a few days—sometimes hours. Mindfulness is not like that. You can't "make" it happen and it won't come in a few sessions. The secret is that if you do put your mind toward finding the right kind of mindfulness practices for your life, you will find the ideal solution. No, it isn't immediate, but if you set your mind to finding it and the configuration that works for you, the benefits are plentiful.

"If you focus on enlightenment, you practice mindfulness."

Meditation and mindfulness got bad names because of their assumed affiliation with enlightenment. Not that there is anything wrong with enlightenment, but it doesn't always have the positive connotation that true users value. Here, though, mindfulness meditations have little to do with enlightenment. In fact, it can be highly practical and create benefits that show up in your daily life. If you're seeking enlightenment, you'll find it. On the other hand, if you just want to be calmer and more at peace, hold the enlightenment stuff—you can easily find that, too.

As you can see, much misinformation is out there about the art of mindfulness. In many ways, these ideas have stripped it of its power. What you must realize is that most of them are incorrect ideas that are detrimental to the growth and popularity of this method of understanding the world.

Now that we have covered what mindfulness isn't, let's start learning exactly what it is!

CHAPTER 4

Where You Want to Be

Now that we're easing up on what mindfulness really is, let's cover where you want to be. Likely, regardless of your life situation, you want to be more balanced. When you realize the benefits of being mindful, you'll start to see why so many people are committed to it. There are three benefits of practicing mindfulness regularly:

- Mental clarity and well-being
- Better physical health
- Better emotional health

Research has proven that mindfulness can positively affect your entire life. Don't think that being mindful will take hours and hours of your time, either. Even finding a few moments here and there throughout your life can reap innumerable benefits for you. The fact is, when you learn to be mindful, you are teaching your mind to operate in a different way. You are teaching it to slow down, focus and be in the "now." It may take some time to get there, but the benefits of being mindful throughout your day will show themselves as you practice. Let's look at each of the above three and see exactly what this practice can help you with.

CHAPTER 5

Mental Clarity/
Well-Being

Mindful meditation is the key to improving your mental clarity. Overall, your cognitive abilities will improve, as studies have shown. As stated earlier, our ancestors realized the benefits early on, but now we have the technology to prove it. Both the MRI and the EEG show changes that appear and the neurological benefits. A recent study showed that patients who performed a regular meditative process had more "gray matter volume" throughout the brain. What is this? Well, gray matter volume refers to the area of the brain's neuronal cells. This area controls your memory, your emotions, your decision-making skills, your self-control and your muscle control. Just think of meditation as a means of boosting the control you have over your body. Even older patients showed marked signs of improvement as compared to same-aged patients who didn't practice mindfulness. Overall, it offers benefits regardless of the age of the subject.

Harvard University conducted a study in 2011 that showed some interesting results. As directed by Professor Sara Lazar, the study concluded that neural systems are definitely modifiable networks and changes within them can occur through consistent training. This information was groundbreaking because of what it meant. Formerly, people believed that you "get what you get" in terms of brain function. Yes, you can study to increase your informational coffer, but the tools your brain actually uses to comprehend it are limited by innate (and unchangeable) ability. What the Harvard study did was prove that this is not true.

Students at the University of Massachusetts Medical School were the test subjects, all of whom were individuals who felt that they needed some form of stress reduction. Each subject was not on any medications, including holistic supplements. The students were given MRIs. Both the sample and a control sample were directed to engage in meditation for a six-week testing period. After the time was over, each subject underwent a second MRI. During the second testing, it was found that the group that participated in meditation came away with increased left hippocampus gray matter content.

Another interesting benefit connecting mental clarity with mindful meditation is the lowered "wandering thought" syndrome. Millions of people complain about not having focus. The reality is that people have millions of thoughts running through their minds at any given second. The brain is an amazingly speedy organ that can contemplate a lot. This is aggravated by the demands of everyday life. Put together, the mind is constantly rushing to understand, contemplate, ruminate and create new ideas. Many people complain about their minds wandering from idea to idea without any set course. This is cause for some people to turn to medicine or diet. What they don't realize is that meditation may be the answer they are looking for. Mind-wandering is chronic among people today and it makes life that much harder for those people who must focus intently on one project. A study by Yale University proved that mindful meditation was able to decrease the brain's mind-wandering proclivity. If you have ever thought to yourself, 'I wish I could dial my mind down a few notches," this may be the simplest and healthiest solution for you.

Some people are worried that incorporating this type of focus into their daily or weekly schedules will not affect their outcomes. They think that meditating must happen over the course of years—even decades—to show any vital improvement in cognitive function. One study found that people who practice it for just a few weeks show signs of improvement in both memory and focus. Here's why. When meditating, you learn to focus your mind on one thing and block out other sensations and thoughts. As the core activity, this is difficult, but with intention and practice, you can find success. Your brain doesn't know that it is only practicing this during meditation. Your brain thinks that this is your way of teaching it something new. As with anything it learns, the brain looks for ways to apply the new knowledge. In this case, when the brain addresses other topics— at work, at home, at play—it uses the focus skill to delve deeper into the action at hand.

Don't think that mindfulness is just for adults. Many schools throughout the U.S. have been exploring the effectiveness of mindfulness as combined with the normal school curriculum. In fact, a school district in San Francisco is testing a meditation program that brings its higher-risk children through a twice-daily session. They are reporting decreases in suspensions, increases in student attendance and increases in overall GPAs. Some medical experts are suggesting that incorporating a mindfulness schedule within young people may be the key to improving their still-developing brains and maximizing their eventual adult mind power.

Finally, meditation with a focus on being mindful may help with the chronic "me" syndrome. Today's technology-based world is highly centered on what people need and giving them the ability to receive it within seconds. Whether they are looking for directions, a new outfit, a specialized item or even food, they can use the internet to find it within seconds and make a qualified decision about what they want. This immediacy is changing the face of young people who never had to live within evolving technology like older generations did. It is creating a very self-centered "me" world. People complain about younger generations and their me-centricity, but what can be done to help with the issue? Meditation can break the "me" pattern and help both adults and children look beyond themselves and their own patterns. It helps them see the bigger picture—which rarely, beyond the psychopathic mind, is accessible—with deliberate seeking.

Overall, meditation is a huge benefit for people's mental abilities and cognitive well-being. With as few as two weekly sessions for six weeks required to see true change, it is one of those activities that has enough benefits that using it is a no-brainer. This is just one of the major ways meditation can contribute to your quality of life. Let's look at your overall physical health next and what meditation mindfully can do for it!

CHAPTER 6

Better
Physical Health

The body takes on a lot of stress throughout our lives. Close your eyes and reflect on your day. Picture what you do on any given day and think about everything your body tackles. Now is a great time to say a big "thank you" for everything and come up with ways you can help your body. Mindful meditation is a key tool for improving overall physical health.

A study done earlier this year by the NCCIH, or the National Center for Complementary and Integrative Health, showed that mindfulness can help control both acute and chronic pain without using the brain's opiates. It is believed that anywhere from 20 to 30 percent of the world's population has some sort of chronic pain. This goes well beyond a minor injury or temporary discomfort. Normally when a patient feels pain, his or her brain releases a natural opiate that eliminates the brain's ability to perceive pain.

There are two primary causes of chronic pain:

1)   *nerve damage and*

2)   *a physical cause.*

Both can be so harrowing that they trick the brain into believing that pain is standard. Over time, the brain develops its own skill of wrongly interpreting a wide range of inputs as pain. This misinformation and inaccurate interpretation can cause other issues. Imagine having to manage life and all its activities while managing pain every waking moment. Without the ability to distinguish between chronic and acute pain, the brain is subject to receiving more intense pain signals regardless of the cause—even if the cause is relatively minor.

Meditation and being mindful can also help sustain your brain and bypass the effects of aging. The thing about aging is that everyone goes through it. There is nothing you can do to stop it—it will happen. We have all seen people who are fighting it tooth and nail with cosmetic surgeries, ointments, elixirs, etc. They want to find that one magic cure that will put their aging on hold. Guess what? Though some people may experience improvement in their skin tone or demeanor because of various treatments, those minutes keep ticking. There is nothing that can stop the aging process. However...

New research is showing that you can affect the brain's aging process through meditation. A UCLA study found that people who incorporate meditation into their daily routines have much better-preserved brains when they reach their older years. As people age, a loss of volume within the brain is normal. However, the study showed that those with mindfulness benefited by having a greater and younger volume. The interesting thing was that the volume wasn't limited to the area of the brain formerly associated with meditating. Rather, a widespread maintenance of volume within the brain presented itself in long-time meditators. In addition, a Harvard study found that after eight weeks of mindful meditation, cortical thickness was increased. That's the part of the brain that supports memory and learning.

Mindfulness can positively affect the body directly. One of the key aspects of being mindful is to slow down one's breathing, which in turn slows down the heart rate. Imagine the last time you were in a stressful or anxious situation. It may have caused your breathing to quicken and put more stress on your cardiovascular system. Repeatedly, this can damage your system and create lasting negative effects. Being mindful slows down the cardiovascular system, giving it a break from the harrowing day it takes you through. Usually, about two-thirds of participants in a mindfulness exercise class experience lowered blood pressure by the end as a response to relaxation. After three months, this lowered cardiovascular exertion becomes normal even when a person is not meditating.

Diseases and stroke are also targets for mindfulness. A study done in 2012 looked at individuals who were considered high-risk for heart disease and who were asked to engage in either better dietary practices and exercise or mindful meditation. They were followed for the next three years. Among those who meditated regularly, 48 percent saw a reduction in their telltale symptoms. The changes were heavily tied to the slowing of their heart rates, which in turn lowered psychosocial stresses and blood pressure.

According to Medical News Today, a recent study showed that mindfulness can also affect rheumatoid arthritis and asthma. The belief is that psychological stressors play a large role in the occurrence of both, or at a minimum exacerbate their effects. The University of Wisconsin tested that theory. It created a mindfulness-based stress-lowering program designed for patients suffering from either asthma or arthritis. Patients were targeted if they had chronic and consistent pain. They were told to focus on their breathing, both sensations and mental content while meditating. What the university found was that behavioral interventions created to reduce emotional reactivity benefit people suffering from forms of chronic pain and chronic inflammation.

In addition to the many benefits cited above, the body sees other benefits from mindful meditation. Here are some of the most profound:

Lessens brain problems
Lessens inflammatory disorders
Lessens premenstrual and menopausal issues
Helps prevent fibromyalgia
Improves the energy level
Improves the immune system
Improves the resting heart rate
Reduces the blood pressure

The bottom line is that if you are looking for true longevity and maintaining your body's youthfulness for as long as possible, mindfulness will help you. Your physical body is important—without it, you are at risk of suffering from a variety of pains that are considered part of the aging process. If you could bypass that or at least minimize the effects of growing older, why wouldn't you? Here is where you can be proactive with a tool that not only serves your body but offers a complete and obvious benefit from head to toe.

CHAPTER 7

Better
Emotional Health

D on't think that mindfulness is helpful only with your mental clarity and physical well-being. In fact, it can help your overall emotional health. Millions of people throughout the world are seeking help with managing their emotions. Some go overboard and are over-emotional; others never show emotions. Either way, they are having issues with managing their emotions. Others have imbalances that make moderation impossible. A steady schedule that incorporates mindfulness can help with this also.

Depression is a widespread problem in today's world. It's no wonder. Depression is estimated to affect more than 19 million Americans, or about 10 percent of the U.S. population. A recent study showed that throughout their lives, about 10 to 25 percent of all women and about 5 to 12 percent of men will suffer from some form of lasting clinical depression. Studies also show that the risk of suffering from depression increases with age, although the elderly suffer less often from major depression. There is hope, though!

A recent study held at five middle schools in Belgium proposed a plan for engaging their students in mindfulness programs. The 400 students participating, aged between 13 and 20 years old, all showed signs of decreased stress, anxiety and depression. They were compared to the students who did not participate in the study. The findings were supported by another study done at the University of California, in which patients with depression agreed to participate in a mindfulness meditation class throughout a six-month period. They too felt better and saw a lessened occurrence of depressive feelings and mood changes. What the studies are proving is that mindfulness can be a secondary form of anti-depression drug therapy.

Another group prone to emotional changes and that can fall into depression is pregnant women. They report a higher risk because of the emotional ups and downs that pregnancy can create. Some hospitals are encouraging women to participate in mindfulness yoga and meditation classes. They showed a clear reduction in the symptoms of depression among expectant mothers. Not only do they reap the overall physical benefits of the practice, but the mothers' depression is lessened. This, in turn, allows them to bond with their babies more readily, without depression to manage on top of their pregnancies.

Basically, anything that promotes intense negative emotion can be targeted by mindful meditation. The American Journal of Psychiatry reported that patients who were diagnosed with either panic disorders or anxiety disorders benefited from programs focusing on mindfulness. Panic attacks are characterized by:

- Heart pounding and accelerated heart rate
- Trembling
- Sweating
- Shortness of breath
- Chest pain
- Feelings of choking
- Nausea
- Dizziness
- Chills
- Numbness
- Fear of losing control
- Fear of dying

Overall, panic attacks can cause trauma to the sufferer, making them afraid of experiencing life. Without a true solution, this can create a life of terrifying experiences. The good news is that there are proactive ways to calm the effects of a panic attack. By creating a schedule of mindful meditation, people find that instances of panic attacks and anxiety decrease. If they do feel a panic attack coming on, they learn the tools to return to a calmer state. It takes practice, but it does work for some people. The value of mindfulness is that it isn't merely an extraneous act that you must schedule into your life. Rather, it offers real-life benefits for actual medical issues. Anyone who has suffered a panic attack knows how difficult they can be to manage. Once a person is in them, they are debilitating. Having the tools needed to, at a minimum, quell the anxiety level can be invaluable to someone suffering from these attacks.

Studies have also shown that being mindful can assist with eating disorders and substance abuse problems. The key, as doctors state it, is that mindfulness requires people to accept the experiences they have gone through—good and bad. Addressing those painful emotions that exacerbated or triggered their disorders can help the patients manage them. Some specialists agree that mindful work is a better option than avoidance or aversion therapy, which are sketchy in their results at best. Doctors combine practices of mindfulness with cognitive behavioral therapy and psychotherapy. They all help people gain control and maintain perspective on irrational, harmful, self-defeating and maladaptive thoughts.

As a proactive and easy-to-carry-out action, it makes sense to try!

CHAPTER 8

What Exactly is Mindfulness?

N
ow that we've covered the benefits of mindfulness, what it isn't and what it can affect, let's discuss what it truly is! It is important that you put away your preconceived notions or the idea that mindfulness is an exclusive process for the spiritually minded. As we covered earlier, it is beneficial to all people on many levels. Yes, it can be a spiritual bonus to your soul, but it can also offer a practical advantage to your everyday life.

Mindfulness is maintaining a constant instant-by-instant awareness of our feelings, bodies, thoughts and environment. It is focusing on the "now" and being acutely aware of your state of being at this very moment. It may sound odd. Again, the brain processes millions of thoughts every minute. They fire wildly like a machine gun. This is the result of a busy day and how quickly the brain can work. Finding a way to quiet all that down and focus on "now" is where it all starts.

Mindfulness involves a variety of tools:

Body senses.

You'll notice things more in depth as your body experiences them. Possibly when you are being mindful, you'll notice an itch or a reflex within your body. You'll let them pass as you continue to focus.

The senses.

Your senses of seeing, hearing, tasting, touching and smelling will all be utilized to their maximum capacity. Mindfulness is about paying attention to each of these and experiencing what they have to offer you.

Your emotions.

You'll also feel emotions as you focus on different thoughts. Let them come, acknowledge them and let them go. Remember to keep all judgment out of your mindful work. Let what happens happen in a judgment-free zone.

Surfing.

When you quiet down, your body may suddenly experience things it wants— a cup of coffee, a snack, a bathroom break, etc. Try to quell these thoughts so you can stay on track and focus.

General meditative benefits.

As you practice mindfulness, you will see an increased ability to meditate more regularly and with more intent. The very act of being mindful teaches your brain to focus, and that focus will branch out to all experiences.

Acceptance

First, with mindfulness, it is important to accept your thoughts. The fact is, we go through millions of thoughts, so the natural result is that we label many of them as being "good" or "bad." Let's say you start thinking about your bills. You may subconsciously think of this as a "bad" thing. You have a mortgage payment, a car payment and a utility bill payment due this week and you'll have to make those payments, thus seeing a diminished bank account. Since you became an adult you have been going through the process, and the act of paying bills is not a "good" one. It creates stress and fear, along with anxiety and loss.

One of the first tasks you must address when getting on the road to mindfulness is to change your "good" and "bad" labels. The fact is, you can experience something and label it "good" while someone the same age and from the same neighborhood can label the exact same experience "bad." What does that tell us?

It tells us that things are not easily labeled "good" or "bad." It's always subjective. Recall the bill payment example used earlier. Instead of thinking about bill payment as "bad," what if you thought of it as a great way to get the things you love? For example, you pay your mortgage and that allows you to put a roof over your head and your family's heads. They get to experience life as a family together in one space and be joyous about the time spent there. You work hard to create holidays and weekends so your family can have an enjoyable time. How are you able to do that? With your monthly mortgage payment. When framing the issue of paying your mortgage like this, it is no longer a "bad" thing to pay it. Rather, it is an exchange that allows you to have something invaluable.

When you work with mindfulness, you will be addressing your thoughts, and it is important to stop labeling them as "bad." Here's the thing about labels—they happen subconsciously and then attach themselves to everything. You likely categorize things as "good" or "bad" all day and then feel accordingly. What you must realize is that your labeling is not a superficial categorization. It is telling your brain and your body how to react to certain occurrences. You want to get rid of the labels.

Detach yourself from the labeling process. How do you rework a habit? Usually, you must address the habit, form a new replacement habit and then practice it. Go down the list of things you consider "bad." Here are some:

"The drive to work is bad because of all the traffic!"
"My boss is a dictator who doesn't listen to anyone."
"My coworkers are busybodies."
"Lunch options around my workplace are bad!"
"My kids never listen and aren't ready in the morning."
"My spouse doesn't help me get the kids ready in the morning."
"My best friend doesn't respect my time!"
"I pay bills, but it sucks to dish out that much money!"
"I don't have enough time in the day for anything I want to do!"
"I can't get a few minutes at night to relax."

Have you ever heard yourself saying things like this to yourself or your friends? Think about other situations in which you made negative statements like these. You automatically have a situation in mind and have labeled it. Of course, these are all things that are common in today's world; millions of people deal with each one of them. As you embark on your mindful meditation lifestyle, you will want to address your feelings. Ask yourself what your true preconceived notions about life are. Here is a great time to sit down and do some thinking. Write down all the notions you have about life—anything you label "bad." The first step to changing your thought process is realizing it, acknowledging it and being honest about it.

Once you have your list of thoughts, start going through each one and try to reframe it. For example, from the list above take "My coworkers are busybodies!" Think about what a better option would be to address this issue. Get away from the "good" or "bad" label. Just think about the truth. Here are the truths that first come to mind with this statement:

You must work with people.

The people you work with behave in a way you don't like.

Looking at the first one, you must work with people. That is a reality. Whether you're living in a big city or on a rural farm, you must deal with people on some level for the exchange of goods and services. This is the only truth to that statement. Is it good? Is it bad? It doesn't matter what label you give it—it still is. Looking at the second one, you aren't happy with how the people in your office behave. The bottom line is that you can't change them. People change on their own agenda and not without much personal effort. What you can do, however, is remove yourself professionally from the dialogue that you believe makes them "busybodies." If you're removed from the furor, the label can be eliminated. You don't have to think about the label as bad and you don't need all the feelings associated with that label. Maybe as a result of thinking about your coworkers as "busybodies," you are hesitant to share in their stories. Maybe you feel intimidated by their intent. Regardless, you can remove yourself, do your job and socialize without the culprits.

So, why is it important to sort through your preconceived notions of "good" and "bad"? The action of subconsciously labeling things is a prevalent one. We develop it early. Just think about the times your parents told you something was "good" or "bad." We grow accustomed to those labels and then rely on them as we get older. When you are a child, they work—they let you know what is acceptable and what isn't. Even an 18-month-old baby understands "no." Whether the child listens is a completely different story, but he or she gets the message that whatever he or she is doing is not permitted.

The damage of these labels is that when we have thoughts, we learn to label them too. This judgment extends to our own thoughts and can cause us to judge ourselves based on them. With mindfulness, you will purposely be more aware of your thoughts than ever before. Because of this, you must do some work on getting rid of the habit of labeling them. Recall the example of paying your mortgage? Learn to reframe the auto-thought to the good thing about paying your mortgage. If you can do this with tangible things in your life, you can train your mind to continue this lack of judgment when addressing the intangible thoughts that come and go.

Practice

Second, when it comes to mindfulness, you must practice. Just think about playing tennis. You could reasonably pick up a racket and start playing. You may need a quick tutorial on the game play and rules, but you could do it relatively easily within a few minutes. However, that doesn't mean you'd be doing it well. The bottom line is that the Serena Williamses and Bjorn Borgs of the world are veterans who have played for decades. In fact, most of the best players started when they were toddlers. It has taken decades of practice for them to get to the level at which they are. They have failed millions of time and missed millions of serves. What made them different is that though they failed, they kept pushing forward and returning to the court. Mindfulness is the same!

As you know, the mind goes through billions of thoughts. The ability to slow all that down is not an easy one to attain. Your brain is used to working on super-speed from morning to night. It is used to seeing one thing and making decisions about what to do next. For example, your brain smells coffee in the morning. It makes the decision to get you out of bed, get your robe on, get your slippers on, get you down the stairs, get a coffee cup, add creamer, add sugar, add coffee and stir. That's just from one smell! Your brain makes a succession of decisions based on that, and that's one of the simplest examples of what your brain processes throughout any given hour. In fact, this is one of the simplest things your brain is trained to process during any given hour.

When you want to do something contradictory to what you're used to, it takes practice. Mindfulness is a purposeful intention to focus on the now—to become more focused on your body, your thoughts and emotions. As discussed earlier, the practice helps you on many levels—mental, physical and emotional. However, it isn't easy to incorporate a new habit into your life. Here are three steps that can help you build any new desired habit:

Commit to it for 30 days. Studies show that it takes this long to make an action automatic. Of course, it depends on how entrenched you are in the old habit, but a 30-day stint of remembering to do it is a great place to start.

Start slowly. Particularly at the beginning it may be difficult, but that's why you can start at the pace you want.

Don't try to jump into mindfulness full-throttle the first week. Have a two-week check-in. Mark your start date on the calendar and in two weeks give yourself a check-in. Stay aware of what works for you and what doesn't. Make any changes necessary for success.

Although it will take time to get into the habit of mindfulness, you can do it. The bottom line is that the benefits are enormous and you'll like the results you get once you are on a good schedule.

If you need any proof of the usefulness of mindfulness, consider the following testimonials:

> *"I rush all day from morning to the wee hours of the night. Taking a few minutes to be aware of life as it is right now is key for my sanity." ~Tricia, Atlanta, GA*
> *"I was introduced to mindfulness when I was in my teens but didn't realize its value until I got into life as a true adult. That's when finding time to center was crucial." ~Carl, St. Petersburg, FL*
> *"Being aware of the now saved me from a lot of wasted time. I finally purposely found time for me." ~Jamie, Tucson, AZ*
> *"Mindful meditation added immeasurably to my sanity. I work two jobs and have a lot of hobbies so down-time needs to be maximized!" ~Ed, San Francisco, CA*
> *"With mindfulness I learned how to slow down my life and focus. The thing about it is that it doesn't just benefit [you] while you're meditating. It helps you focus more at work and at home too." ~Tony, Memphis, TN*

The bottom line is that people from every walk of life, every age, every demographic can practice mindfulness and learn to be more centered. One thing that those who already practice it agree on is that its value seeps into other parts of their lives. This isn't just a stand-alone time when you focus on yourself. You will literally be training your brain to focus, and this focus helps you while you're working on other aspects of your life. You will be able to segment a project at work or at home and truly focus on it without all the extra noise with which you normally struggle. It is important to remember that when you are practicing being mindful, it takes time to develop the skills to maintain it, but in the end, the return is invaluable.

CHAPTER 9

Preparing For Mindfulness

Becoming more mindful is a process. The good news is that you are free to practice mindfulness anytime, anywhere. You can do it through a variety of activities. Meditation, mindful moments and body scans are all ways of reaching into your mindfulness practice. Here are some tips to get you started when you're ready for the process.

The Planning

First of all, be ready to set aside some time for yourself. When you start the process, you may hear that you need a special cushion or a special tool. If you do a Google search, you'll find thousands of experts who suggest different tools to use. They'll have an entire plan for you to get started. They will also suggest that if you purchase their tools, you'll be that much more successful. Now, you can explore the things out there to help you center, but if you want to test out mindfulness, you really need absolutely nothing. All you must do is clear out a time in your day when you can quiet yourself and practice. To come up with some time is the challenge for busy people. Ask yourself the following:

Do I get other people ready in the morning?
Do I work full-time or part-time?
Do I work during the day or at night?
What do I do during my current downtime?
What is critical and time-sensitive?
What can I negotiate out of my schedule?
The ending question is: What can I do, delegate or delete?

The goal is to look at your life and find what you can shift. Studies show that people who are busy almost always have things they can alter. The problem is, they get so used to doing "everything" that they don't have time to assess their lives. This is a great time to get that process going. Start by making a list of all the things you must work with throughout the week. Take your non-negotiable items, such as work, children's activities, appointments, etc., and log them on your calendar. When you're done, consider the other items—your negotiables. This is when you want to use the ending question: What can I do, delegate or delete?

Go through your negotiable list and ask this question. If you can do it, schedule it on your calendar once, or a few times if it is a big project. The goal is to get it off your to-do list. For example, let's say you mark Saturday afternoons from 1 p.m. until 4 p.m. for cleaning your garage. The problem is that this has been on your calendar for the past two months but things have continuously come up to push your schedule off target. Put it into your calendar and commit to it. If you get it done when you scheduled it, you won't have to look at it again. That's free time you can use to do things for yourself, one of which is to engage in mindfulness.

Let's say you have it on your weekly calendar to clean your nine- and 10-year-olds' bedrooms. Maybe you have them do the major cleaning, but you like to go behind them and make sure they put everything in place...and you fix it when they don't. At nine and 10 years old, your kids are ready to take that responsibility upon themselves. Learn to delegate that space to their care. You can check afterward, but commit to spending no more than 15 minutes total on your part of keeping them organized. If it takes more than that, you can schedule time with them individually to teach them how to better organize and clean.

Finally, you will hopefully find some things on your list of to-dos that are ready for deletion. These are simple because they immediately open space for you to start practicing other, more valuable things, like mindfulness.

After you complete this exercise, you can look at your schedule to see the actual free time you have. Hopefully, you'll walk away with a better timeline and have opened the door to truly bringing mindfulness into your life. Once you have your schedule, you're ready to move on to the second part of the process.

Being Present

Second, you want to learn how to be present. This is another skill that takes time to learn. So many people spend their time in the future. They think about what they must do later today, tomorrow, next week, next month...they also think about what their friends, boyfriend, spouse, children, family members must do in the future. The average person today must manage work, home, family, friends and free time. To do that takes a lot of planning. No one can take that away from you and most people must plan throughout their days. The thing about being present, though, is that you want to eliminate these thoughts.

The key to mindfulness is learning to focus on the present and to stay there. If you're having problems with this, which you likely will, here are some tools you can use to help:

Use your planning time wisely. If you have a time of the day or week when you do your major planning, start using it wisely. Most professionals use Monday mornings as their plan time. They consider who they must see, what they must do and what their goals are for the week. Parents may use the weekend to do their planning for their families and children. It is important that you discipline yourself to do your planning during this time and not during your mindfulness time. If you find yourself focusing on the future and what to do during your mindfulness time, remind yourself that you already took care of what you could. Re-center yourself to the now.

Get organized. Another tool you can use to give yourself power over your "thoughts on the future" is to get and stay organized. Again, you want to embark on the journey of mindfulness and that means clearing out the unnecessary things you tackle throughout the day. Recall the housecleaning earlier? Where you practiced writing down things you must do, separating them into negotiables and non-negotiables? The value is that you'll enter your mindfulness and know with confidence that you have taken care of all you can to ensure that your future is as planned-out as possible. Once you have this confidence, you'll be able to set aside some of those wandering thoughts about the future. If a thought jumps to the forefront of your mind, you can remind yourself that you have it covered. You can re-center yourself on the present and continue your mindfulness technique.

Recall the "do, delegate, delete"? Start doing it! As you clear your schedule, you'll find the "dos," the "delegates" and the "deletes." You have already gone through your list of things to do and have categorized them. Hopefully, you also got onto the task of categorizing them into the three headings above. Once you do, you can remind yourself that everything is taken care of. Some people like to write down any "final thoughts" right before they start their mindfulness session. When you first settle yourself, you will likely have thoughts that come to your mind. Getting over the hump of quieting them will take practice. Sometimes writing them down beforehand is the answer. Other times, soft music can help. In some cases, simply centering your focus on one thing in the room can help. With time, you'll test the different tools and find those that work the best for you. Don't be afraid to reach out and test things. Part of mindfulness is being open to your needs and understanding what you want.

Have a go-to tool to help you focus. This is a tie-in to the last tip. If you take on the task of learning how to be mindful, you will seek tools that keep you centered. Your goal is to keep trying things. Keep track of what works and what doesn't. Remember that millions of people are embarking on the same journey and they are all likely using different tools to achieve the same goal. One tip is to use visualization. If a thought about the future comes rushing to you, picture it in your mind floating off into space and then bring yourself back to "the now." Again, test different tools. The good news is that mindfulness is a process and a lifelong pursuit. You have the rest of your time, and as you develop, so will the tools you use to stay present. If you find that a tool isn't as useful as it once was, look for others. Seek and you will find—that's a maxim that works with mindfulness too!

Give yourself time to learn how to use these tools. One thing you will quickly realize is that mindfulness is a process you must ease yourself into. Most people can't let go of constant thoughts about the future without concerted effort. Let's face it; we are programmed to focus on the future. Just think about the commercials, print ads and radio ads you listen to daily. The media wants to plan your future for you and reminds you of that fact every moment you're listening to or reading it. Find tools that work for you and that help you quiet down the "noise" of the future so you can reach true mindfulness.

Staying Present

Third, recall that the goal of mindfulness is to be in the present moment. There are a lot of misunderstandings when it comes to the term "mindfulness." Some people believe that the goal is to reach a state of complete calm. They recall seeing television programs or gurus talk about it and think that it is an odd state of peace. They may think it means sitting cross-legged on the floor while wearing a robe.

Those are two examples of what it isn't! Mindfulness is when you make yourself acutely aware of your life right now and eliminate any judgment. This is the key to the process.

Remember talking about "good," "bad" and "labeling"? This is where your ridding yourself of the labeling process will benefit you. Judgment is great...if you're a judge. If you aren't, you must let go of the harshness of judgment and be open. In particular, with mindfulness work, you want to leave judgment out of the activity. You go through thousands of thoughts at any given moment, so being impartial is critical. Also remember that at first you likely won't be good at it. You'll become aware of a thought and immediately note a self-judgment afterward. It inevitably swoops in and takes its usual place. Again, this is normal.

The difference this time, though, is important to the mindfulness process. When you sense a judgment, you want to acknowledge it and then move on. Pretend your judgment is a four-year-old who hasn't had a nap. The child is cranky. He or she is difficult. The child makes snap decisions. Have you ever put a piece of candy in front of a four-year-old? He or she likely immediately take the candy with eyes lighting up. The child's judgment was that it's "good." What if you put dirty plates in front of a four-year-old? The child already knows that's "bad" and likely won't take them from you. What would you do with either response? Likely you would let the child make the judgment and move on. Do the same thing with your own judgments. Let them happen, then move on. Never validate them or offer much more than a superficial acknowledgment of them.

The key to "moving on" is to do some mental picturing. One tool is to literally picture your thought in your hand and then your hand opening to release the thought. Mentally picture it floating out of your hand and up to the sky. Hopefully, you'll have to do this only a few times before your mind starts understanding the goal. You're telling your mind that the labeling is ok, but it is unimportant. Eventually, when your mind realizes the labeling is unimportant, it will help you start letting it go altogether. Again, though, this is another thing that will take some time. You will find that as your mind gets used to the idea that it isn't important or valuable to label things, it will stop readily doing so.

With mindfulness, you want to learn to pull yourself back to the center. Some people like to start with a mindfulness course. They believe that an instructor helps them manage challenges like re-centering. Of course, for some this can work. But the honest truth is that you can do this by yourself relatively easily. The value of doing it by yourself is that you can squeeze it into your day on your terms, without having to coordinate times with anyone else or schedule a class. If you have a few moments in the morning before everyone else is up, you can do it then. If you have time in the parking lot at work when you arrive, you can do it then. If you have time late at night, that's fine. Here are some methods of managing mindfulness and re-centering:

Diffuse the inner talk. Sometimes the drama of life crops up when you get a free moment. If that free moment is scheduled when you want to practice mindfulness, this can be a problem. Drama can be a fly buzzing around you. The bottom line is that drama and life will not stop, even for those who are being mindful. You may have a great history of quelling thoughts at first and then, in a few months, lose that ability. If your stress level heightens, it is only natural that it will seep into your free time. Some people embark on a life of practicing mindfulness, but they already have a life of practicing worrying. This is a great swap, but it will take effort to make it happen. What works for some people is to have time to address that "drama" time. Literally schedule time for your brain to address it. This is a tool that helps you train your brain to understand when it is time to deal with problems and when it is time to deal with drama. This works well for some purposeful mindfulness participants, in particular, those who have a lot on their plates and find calmness difficult to achieve.

Relax. Some people think that relaxation happens when they sit down, or when they go to bed at night. They think that relaxation and not moving are synonymous—they aren't. You can lay down at night and have millions of thoughts. You can lay down at night and require minutes, even hours, to achieve true relaxation. It is important to figure out what works for you in terms of relaxation. Some people like to practice mindfulness in the morning, sitting on the couch. Others like to practice it when they are outside in nature. Your setting isn't important. You just want to try a few areas to find out what works best for you. Usually, avid mindfulness-lovers use breathing as a means of bringing on the relaxed state. They start with a few deep breaths, then slow down their breathing. In turn, this slows down the heart rate and creates a greater sense of calm within the entire body. It helps to truly bring on the relaxed state needed to continue focusing on the "now." Again, test things to find the setting that helps you achieve and maintain relaxation.

Anticipate stress and thoughts. Here's the thing about taking time out of your schedule to be mindful—once you do it, you'll free up time for practicing it. Your brain doesn't naturally leave behind all the stress and thoughts of the day. In fact, your brain is accustomed to holding onto those thoughts and fixing them as best it can. Your brain isn't used to just letting go and centering itself. It has gone through a lifetime of jumping from numerous thoughts to more and even more. You can be sure that stress and meandering thoughts will crop up. This is natural and to be expected. Don't worry about it, though. Millions of people experience the same thing, but remember the tool for these thoughts— acknowledge them, let them go and re-center.

Stay grounded. Just like everything else, staying grounded is a habit you must work on developing. And, yes, just like other habits, it can take 30 days to get into your schedule and on your brain's radar. When you consider someone who is grounded, what do you think about? They are likely not easily moved from their intent; they are calm, they are not agitated by their surroundings, they are flexible and accepting of things they don't necessarily want. How do you think they got to that point? Likely some of it was their natural proclivity, but some of it was their purposeful intention. Ask them about their mindset and see if you can adopt some characteristics that will help you stay grounded. One of the main goals of practicing mindfulness is to continue improving your experience and your life. This means that you are open to periodically self-assessing yourself and being honest about what works and what does not work. This will help you continue growing as a person and learning what being mindful truly is.

This may seem like a lot of preparation to be mindful. And, yes, it is! However, it is necessary to know what you're embarking on. Mindfulness is not an immediate solution. It isn't like the internet or your mobile device. It is a long-term commitment that will appreciate in value as you continue practicing it.

CHAPTER 10

Getting Started

Now that we've covered what mindfulness is, let's cover its practical uses. Have you ever met someone only to forget their name moments later? Have you ever driven somewhere and honestly not remembered getting there? Have you ever gone to work only to focus on your kids all day? Or vice-versa? All these examples are centered around not being "here." You are there, but your mind is elsewhere. It is normal and most people experience the same thing. Is it the best thing to do with your time?

The bottom line is that you have only 24 hours every day to make the most of it. That means it is important to focus on those moments and experience them—on a deep and profound level. You want to go somewhere and remember it. Think about this past week and how much you experienced but about which you can't recall the specific details. The truth is, most people move through life on auto-pilot. They get the job done, but their minds are already five steps ahead, thinking about what they want to finish tomorrow, or next week, or next year. This robs us of the true and genuine experience that is life.

The way to combat this is to learn how to apply mindfulness to every situation. Learning to focus your attention on the present—the "now" – is what will truly bring value to your world. There are three things that are combined in mindfulness:

Valuing now
Letting go of the past
Letting the future come

Look at those words. Note that the active verb is concerned with only the first one—"valuing." With the others, you just "let" or "allow"—both very passive verbs. All you must do to experience them is let go and relax into them. The first one, the valuing, is where the effort lies. This is what we must focus on and learn how to achieve.

They say that all we can really hold is "now." Think about that. You have three experiences in this world: the past, now and the future. The future is not really in our hands. Yes, we can prepare for it as best we can, but just because you prepare for it doesn't mean it will turn out the way you anticipated. It could be completely different. Just ask the married couple who planned to travel throughout Europe in "a year." They know where they'll go, where they'll stay and what they'll do. They scour the internet to find out exactly what they want to do—from the minutest detail to the biggest sights, they know what their itinerary is from start to finish. They may even start saving for the big trip. Then they have a surprise pregnancy! Their plans are not going to happen right now. They realize that all the effort they put into planning is not going to go the way they anticipated. That isn't to say they won't get to Europe, but they'll be doing it with a little one instead, and likely when the little one is older. It's also not to say their energy was wasted, but it became something completely different from what the couple anticipated.

Or what about the young person who plans to attend a certain college. They build their entire future around their life at an Ivy League school on the east coast. They build their curriculum, their day, they plan their life thousands of miles away. They apply and get accepted. They even have their wardrobe set out and ready to pack. Then they get into a better college on the west coast. The reality is, the future isn't ours to plan. Yes, you can have dreams all you want, but whether they work out the way you envision is not entirely in your hands. It would be nice to order what you want, but that element of surprise is what takes you where you must be at the right time.

What about the energy people put into worrying about the future? Let's say you spend most of this week worrying about next week's bills. Does that help pay them? Or what if you spend countless hours at night worrying about a big project at work due next month? Does that help you create a good result? Of course not! All that energy is wasted. Unfortunately, that is what billions of people do—waste moments worrying. These moments are abundant. And the biggest problem is that no one can ever get them back. Once they are wasted on pointless worrying or fretting over the future, they are gone. You must ask yourself how much good those wasted moments did. This is just another reason why being mindful of the present and staying connected to the "now" is so important.

That is not to even consider the physical, emotional and mental energy it takes to focus on worrying. Most people engage in repeated and chronic wastes of the "now" moments. They are used to it! It is a habit of which they aren't aware, so they don't recognize the need to change. Can anyone really answer the question of when they started worrying? Likely it was as a very young child. They started giving away precious moments to worrying and it quickly became a deeply engrained bad habit—one their parents had, and their parents' parents. Breaking the cycle is an advantage and using mindfulness is the perfect solution to help you become more aware of the "now" and its value.

Next, consider the past. You can spend your entire life regretting something or holding a grudge against someone, but does that change the past? No. Let's say in high school another student embarrassed you. The entire class saw the incident and you have held a grudge against the person for 10, even 20 years. Do your grudge and the energy you put into it do anything for your offense? No, your offense is long gone. The person who orchestrated it probably doesn't even remember it. Even if they do, they have moved on to different things and don't think twice about it.

CHAPTER 11

Steps to
Mindful Meditation

There are six steps you can take to enter a mindfulness meditation. If you have the time to schedule meditation, you can easily guide yourself. Of course, if you're particularly time-strapped, you can try periodic mindfulness throughout the day. If you do find time, you can schedule a block throughout your week, or even day, when you purposefully focus on the process. Here are the steps to engaging in mindful meditation:

Sit upright with a good and comfortable posture.

Cross your legs and keep your gaze lowered. One of the first things you'll realize about meditation is that it doesn't have strict rules. If you feel better with outstretched legs or even lying down, you can easily substitute. However, some research shows that the upright and crossed-leg position is the easiest in which to reach a meditative space. The point is to be comfortable when you begin. Some people wonder about the setting; the great thing about meditation is that it is flexible enough for you to do it just about anywhere. When you first start, it may help you to be at home in a very controlled atmosphere. As you grow more accustomed to it, you can venture out to less-controlled areas and still come away with the same results. The important thing is to ease into it. You know yourself better than anyone and if you're easily distracted, choose a place with minimal interruptions.

Take a few deep, cleansing breaths.

Breathing is a central job of your body. The tie between the two is intimate. Your breathing can speed up your entire body's processes and it can slow them down. It is a central way for you to control how your body is functioning. In fact, it is one of the few ways you can tune into exactly how quickly your body is operating and affect it depending on what outcome you want. This is why when you are meditating you will find that using your breathing helps you slow down and focus. In addition to giving you control of your body, breathing is a great way to center yourself when meditating. Some people have a hard time figuring out how to slow down, and breathing is a tool they find very helpful. Follow your breath as you inhale and exhale. Focus on it until your mind slows down. Likely you will wander off mentally because of the many distractions you face, but you can re-center yourself repeatedly. Also, be sure that when you first start mindful meditation, you set yourself up for success by minimizing distractions as much as you can. This may be difficult, but it will help you stay on center.

Let your thoughts come naturally but remain aware of them.

When you meditate, in particular when you first start, you may find that your mind consistently wanders off. This may be due to a noise you hear or a thought about doing something. It is important that you fend off these thoughts. When you start your mindfulness meditation, expect some resistance. Your mind has been rushing from one thought to another since you were born. It is used to processing millions of sensory experiences since that time, so it isn't used to slowing down. The good news, though, is that with some training, it can learn. One thing many beginners do is try to meditate, wander off and then give up. You must know that a wandering mind is normal. Accept it, take a deep breath and re-center. Try not to judge yourself because this is a difficult thing to grasp at first. Staying on target may elude you for a while. If you have something particularly stressful going on in your life, you may find it more difficult. This is the time when mindful meditation will likely do you the most good, though, so press on. When a thought comes into your mind, allow it to flow, recognize the draw away from attention, acknowledge it without judgment and then return to center.

Learn to categorize your thoughts as "future" or "past."

It is also important to know what your thoughts are as they flow into your mind and to understand which ones should go. To train your brain to focus on the "now," you must give your brain a true reason to focus. Let's say you are being mindful and the thought 'I must cook dinner early because my spouse is coming home early tonight' enters your mind. Acknowledge the thought and recognize that this is a "future" thought. This is your brain wandering to the future to plan it. It is not the "now" you want. Clear it out and start focusing again. Let's say you next have a thought like, 'I didn't like the guy who cut me off in traffic—it still makes me mad to think about it.' Again, acknowledge the thought and recognize it as a "past" thought. Clear it out and start focusing again. Acknowledging thoughts as "future" or "past" is important because this tells your brain that you are not here to deal with either of them right now. Your brain will get it and start to do this automatically. As it categorizes outside thoughts, you can re-center that much quicker. This is the best way to make the most of your mindfulness time.

Keep steadily breathing.

As your thoughts come and you acknowledge and re-center, keep breathing. Your breathing is what you want to center on time and time again. It is also important to keep your breathing steady. Learn to breathe in and out slowly. This is what will slow down your mind and tell your body that it is time to focus on mindfulness. Some people like to use other things to focus on—a flame, a flower, a point in the room, etc. You can easily find something to focus on. Newbies to the world of meditation like to focus on the breath because of how integral it is to the body and how easily it can be focused on. Quieting down your surroundings is important, especially if you are new to the practice. If you find yourself wandering off or your breath changing, re-center yourself and start focusing on a normal breathing rate.

Draw yourself back to center repeatedly.

As you work on your mindful meditation, you will repeatedly have to bring yourself back to center. This is normal. When you first start meditating or if you have a particularly stressful life, you may find that your thought distractions occur much more frequently. This is also normal. Just acknowledge the thought, decide whether it is "future" or "past," let it go and then re-center. The re-centering process will occur time and time again when you begin. When you first start your meditation, you may want to set aside more time to get yourself used to the process. You can look at the first few weeks as a "training period." You will be distracted and have to re-center a lot. As you get more accustomed to it, you'll be able to drop into mindfulness without clearing out the setting for extraneous noises. You'll find that your mind works with you to keep you centered and bring you back to center.

> *Never bring judgment to the meditation session.*

One thing to remember is that wandering thoughts are normal. You will get them. You should never judge yourself. Many newer meditators start the process and almost immediately become inundated with outside thoughts. They get frustrated and end the process, thinking 'I am just not meant for this!' The reality is that no one falls into meditation without some effort. Yes, some people have bigger obstacles to overcome, but everyone can do it. The fact is, you may need a few training sessions to get the hang of it. This is absolutely normal. It is important, though, to keep the area positive, so never let judgment enter the space. There is nothing in this space that should be labeled "wrong" or "bad." Keep it positive so you can find success that much quicker.

Follow the steps to mindful meditation. Remember that there is always room for what feels best to you. If you feel better meditating in the dark, do it. If you feel better meditating with candles, do that. Take some time to find out what works, and what doesn't, for you. There are no rights or wrongs. Let your mind and preferences dictate what method of mindfulness works best for you.

CHAPTER 12

The Importance of the Breath and Mindfulness

The breath and the body are tightly connected to each other. Think about how your breath changes as your day progresses. When you wake in the morning, your breath may be very calm with the in-and-out to which you're accustomed. As you start getting ready for the day, it may speed up. If you have a near-miss in traffic, it may stop momentarily as your heart misses a beat. Your breath is a sign of how your body is responding to the external world.

On top of your breath being connected to your body, it is connected to your emotions. If you're calm, you experience slow, even breathing. If you get agitated or excited, your breath may increase. Think about a time when you were surprised. Likely you drew in a much quicker breath than you did pre-surprise. Emotions tie to breathing and dictate it. The mind is also connected. Your body is an entity that is tied to every part of itself and to the universe.

When you meditate, you re-center to the "now." We talk a lot about the "now." All that means is the essential being you are. Not who you were. Not who you will be. Who you are right "now." The value of centering here is that this is where you are truly connected. Remember that the past is gone. You can't affect it anymore. The future isn't here yet. You can plan it, but whether that plan comes to fruition relies on more than just your planning. The truth is, neither one belongs to you. All you really have is the "now." Learning to focus on it will help you center on all you are and develop your spiritual being.

The bottom line is that the breath is the connective tissue between energy and matter.

It is also a tie between the mind and the consciousness. When you sit with your eyes closed, focused on your breath, you are allowing your mind to become absorbed in that energy and consciousness. When you first begin, you are merely focusing on your normal human breathing; you're focusing on the physical act of breathing. As you continue, you are led to a higher awareness. This higher awareness leads, in turn, to more appreciation, more love, more insight, more of all good things that the spirit-self has.

Many places around the world use the terms "spirit" and "breath" synonymously. Many believe that the spirit is the internal cause of breathing. You can think about meditation using the breath as meditation using the spirit. Both are vitally important to the body—the breath and the spirit. Recognizing their power gives you the chance to harness it for your spiritual betterment.

If you have time to engage in breathing meditation, it is a great way to reach true mindfulness. This is another way to get to the mindful state of mind. Here are the steps you'll take:

Sit in a comfortable but upright position. Place your hands on your thighs with your palms down. It is important to be comfortable because you want to eliminate as many distractions as possible. Taking great care in positioning yourself will help you in the end because you won't have to keep moving. Only you can decide where you want to be. Some people find the floor with a pillow to be the best position; some like the couch and others the bed. Whichever you choose, just like when you're engaging in mindful meditation, make sure you are comfortable.

Turn your eyes downward and close them. There is a reason for turning your eyes downward. This is a trick that helps you lessen distractions and reduce your brain waves. You know all those thoughts that keep rushing through your mind when you try to relax? You can thank your brain waves for that. Research has shown, though, that if you close your eyes, you lessen those raging brain waves by up to 75 percent. If you're practicing mindful meditation, that's exactly what you need. That is exactly the kind of tool that will help you quell some of those thoughts or at least the most intense ones.

Use your nose—not your mouth—to do your breathing. Many people subconsciously use their mouths to breathe. It could be easier if you have allergies

or a cold, but when you're mindfully meditating you want to focus on us
your nose for those deep in-and-out breaths. Be sure your jaw isn't clenche
want your mouth to remain relaxed but closed. You choose your nose as the
breathing tool because it will help continue your focus, as you'll see in the step
below.

Inhale and exhale very deeply and slowly about four times. As you do this,
make sure you are aware of every movement your body makes. This is what
distinguishes this activity from normal meditation. You are mindfully meditating.
You are focused on everything going on "now." You want to pay attention to your
breath. Pay attention to the air as you draw it into your nose. Pay attention to how
the air moves in through your nose and is then guided into your chest. Finally, pay
attention to how it is expelled back out your nose.

One trick is to focus on the nose, the very thing that allows you to move
through this exercise. Realize how your nose feels throughout it. Some people like
to focus on their nostrils and how the air feels as it blows by; other people like to
focus on the tip of their nose. Whichever feels most natural to you is fine. You
want to be completely comfortable throughout the exercise as you strive for
mindfulness. Just keep following the path of air as it moves from the starting
point—your nose—to the end point—your nose.

Let your breathing happen as your relaxed body dictates. You may find that
during one session your breaths are much lighter than others. This is fine. Your
body will change every day and these changes are perfectly acceptable when you
are mindfully meditating. What is important is that you maintain your awareness
the entire time you are focused. Once you center yourself on breathing, be aware
of your entire body as it is in the "now." Let yourself experience everything your
body is going through right "now" and cherish it. Continue breathing and allow
your "now" to flow into your state of mindfulness.

Incoming thoughts and ideas will enter your session of being mindful when
you are meditating. Don't expect to ever have completely uninterrupted
sessions—it sometimes takes years to even get close. What you will learn, though,
is how to re-center and continue the process. When a thought arises in your mind,
be aware of it but detach from it as much as you can. You want to be ambivalent
about any outside stimuli. Your goal is peace, quiet, awareness of the "now" and
energy. By far the most important thing to do is continuously return to a state of
relaxation as you meditate.

If you find yourself at your wits' end with focusing, use these tools to help:

Use the "um" sound to help your mind re-center.

Take a deep, cleansing breath.

Move your head in a circle—front, right side, back and left side, stretching your neck.

Reach your arms over your head as you inhale, then bring them down as you exhale.

Stretch out your legs in front of you.

Lift your arms and shake your hands at the wrists.

Picture something in your mind—a light, a flower, the moon, etc.—and use that to quiet yourself down.

Ultimately, you simply want to re-center yourself on the "now" and these tools can help. Try working with different ones until you find the one that is most useful.

As you engage in mindful meditation, ask yourself some questions periodically. Ask yourself if you are still focused on your nose. Ask yourself if you are still focused on the energy as it moves in and out of your body. Ask yourself if you're focusing on these things from beginning to end of each inhale or exhale. You want to use the entire exercise to help your mind stay in the present state.

Remember that your breath is a way to understand the energy flowing in and out of your body at all times. Sometimes during mindful meditation, you'll find that it is light and soft. Other times it is harder and more uneven. You want to move with it. As you relax, your body will regulate itself. Trust it. There is never a need to force anything when you are practicing mindful meditation. You don't need to control or force it; rather, your job is to experience it in full.

The key element to remember is that the breath is not a "thing" you have. Though you focus on it during your meditation as if it were a "thing," in reality it is a life-sustaining process. It has the power to draw the human engaging in it into a state of higher being. When you become aware of your breath, you are in essence becoming aware of your spirit. Your spirit lives in the "now," which is why mindfulness is so valuable.

Within your body are two levels of breathing—inner and outer. As we learn to mindfully meditate, we use the outer breath to capture our attention and center our minds. When we do this, we slowly move to the inner process of breathing.

This is where spirit takes over and starts to direct us; we understand the spirit-soul consciousness. The reason we envision breathing as both inner and outer is because these actions are reflections of the polarity that exists in everything that is alive. The act of breathing in and out completes the cycle of positive and negative. They are one, but they each move differently.

What is also interesting about using your breath while mindfully meditating is that you must pay attention. Sure, in the beginning, you may find it more difficult, but as you learn how to center yourself, you will find that it is much easier to drop into the "now." Consider that other methods of spiritual growth aren't the same. If you're reciting a mantra, praying or singing, you can still have a wandering mind. If your parents took you to church as a child, how many times did you find yourself mouthing the words to songs or responses while your brain was off thinking about something completely different? It is much more difficult to focus on breathing coming from the nose and to think about something else along with it. Usually, your brain must choose one or the other to truly focus on.

It is also important to realize the power of attention. Attention is the drawing together of thoughts as concentrated on one thing. Science has proven that if you focus on any one thing, you can immediately affect it on some level. In fact, some scientists have stated that they have unintentionally affected an experiment due to their focused attention. The reality is that attention is power. If you can harness that power through your thoughts, you can experience the "now," which is being mindful.

As you continue to practice mindfulness, you will actively notice things. Your practice will help you open your senses and focus on the present. All the mind chatter that drags you forward to the future or backward to the past will slowly ease up. You will likely always feel it on some level, but you will find that as you continue to practice mindfulness, both will subside. When they are at their loudest, you can turn to your mindfulness exercises to get yourself back on track.

CHAPTER 13

Mindfulness for Busy People

Mindfulness is a great tool to have. It keeps your mind centered and focused while giving you a chance to benefit your whole body. For busy people, though, where can you find time to actually do it?

Remember how you looked at your life earlier? The goal was to find those little snippets of time throughout your day and use them. If you can organize your day a little better, you can find time to focus on yourself and your mental well-being. Still not good enough?

Ok, let's get down to business. You have gone through your life. You have written down your negotiable tasks and your non-negotiable tasks. You have sorted out everything as best you can and you realize that an "abundance of free time" just isn't there. First of all, know that you are not alone. There are millions of people who, try as they might, just can't find extra time in their schedules to dedicate to being mindful. Second, know that though mindfulness can be done as a single act, it isn't so greedy that you can't work it into your day while you tackle other things.

Here are some of the easiest ways you can bring the mindful mindset to your day without sacrificing valuable time for other things:

Mindful mini-breaks. If you're looking to really maximize your time and honestly don't have much free time, mindful mini-breaks may be ideal. Remember that the goal of mindfulness is to be present, so you can do that anywhere. If you're at your desk at work and have been working diligently for a few hours, a mindful break can break up the monotony and refresh your mental state. Close all your applications (including the most harrowing one—email) and take a deep breath. You can even try turning away from your computer entirely at this point. Sit for a moment and think about your body—how you feel, what you hear, what's going on around you. The goal is to set aside all thoughts of the past and future and be in the "now" as readily as you possibly can. This is an exercise you can use and take advantage of a few times throughout the day. As you do, you'll find that it gets easier to slip into mindfulness at a moment's notice. You will also learn what works and what doesn't work for you during the process.

Listening mindfully. Any lifelong meditation specialist will tell you that the sounds you hear during meditation can influence the quality of your time. That's why they will tell you to put on soft music or aural sounds if possible. When you're constantly on the go, you probably learn to drown out a lot, but now is when you want to hear those sounds. As you sit quietly, listen to what is going on around you. It could be the office music, trains rushing in the distance or people talking—regardless, focus on it. The key is to learn how to listen to the music without really listening to the lyrics or even the melodies. You want to let its actual sound linger in the background of your mind and help you shut out other thoughts. What is key is to not let your mind wander to thoughts of the future or past. You want to do everything you can to focus on the "now" and stay there. With music, you can try to get wrapped up in the sound and let it flow over you. The goal is to let the music flow over you and to let yourself flow with the music. It may sound difficult but try it. Sometimes music is the key focus you must use to bring yourself back to center and become more mindful.

Nature and mindfulness. Some people have found that nothing brings them a sense of calm like nature. It could be your back porch, a walk to the park, a hike through a forest preserve or a nice bike ride along a river. Whatever is available to you, let your mind calm down and think about what you hear and feel—the light breeze, the sun shining down, the sounds of water rushing, the sounds of the leaves rustling, etc. Whatever you hear, use it as a means of calming your mind and centering yourself. Like other settings, this one may take a few minutes to get into. By far, most people who are longtime mindfulness meditators say that breathing helps calm their minds. We'll talk more about that later, but for now, just believe that you can use it to ease your mind anywhere you go. Nature, with the fresh air it affords, is the perfect place to try it!

Walking meditation. Some people use their lunch hours to take a walk. This is the perfect time to start a walking meditation practice. As long as your walk is more than 10 minutes, you can easily squeeze some brain training time into the day. Some people who use walking for their meditating time focus on the ground under their feet. They focus on the sensations of their feet hitting the ground and the beat. As they do, they let their minds go and start their meditation process. Of course, this is more easily accomplished when there are few distractions. If this is possible, you should choose these routes for your walk, especially when you begin. The key, as usual, is to develop your own sense of relaxed awareness. As you wander, bring yourself back again and again—it will get easier! It is important to never judge yourself if you don't get it "right." With meditation, there is much room for self-expression and "error," though error is really an erroneous term in terms of anything that depends on your personal methodology.

Breathing mindfulness. This is by far one of the most popular ways to reach mindfulness because of how important breathing is. You literally rely on your breathing all day and night. It is something people do completely subconsciously; they rarely put effort into using it proactively. Here is where you can let it shine not only as a life-sustaining activity but as a mind-training one. As you sit comfortably, focus on your breathing. Let your breathing slow down and guide your mind. It is normal for you to wander off, especially when you first begin, but keep centering yourself back to the "now." You want to be sure you are focused. Listening to your own breathing is a great guide that can lead you in the direction you must go. Breathing and mindful meditation are fantastic tools, and there is a whole section on this later. Be sure to complete the exercises to get your mind ready for the benefits of mindfulness.

Mindful eating. Yes, you can take your mealtime as a normally scheduled reminder to practice mindfulness. Some people use their meals as prayer times. You can do the same with meditation. This way you'll automatically be practicing at least three times a day. Again, remember that you don't have to do this for hours on end. A few minutes here and there throughout your day will train your mind. This makes sense—the mind is an amazing thing that works 24 hours a day, seven days a week. It processes, it directs, it makes decisions and it does it at lightning speeds to keep up with your day. Giving it the tools it needs to center itself will be a great benefit. Taking mealtime as a break time is a way to remember your "brain train" breaks. You don't have to stay mindful throughout your entire meal—in fact, that is highly unlikely. However, you want to start with your focused attention. While you're eating, make it a point to be cognizant of your food—the texture, the smell, the taste. Pay attention to what you are ingesting.

Using scented candles to be mindful. There is a reason why people use candles for meditation—they work. Just think about spas and masseurs and how they use candles. The sense of smell is a powerful one and when your brain senses the right smells, you can notify it that the time has come to be mindful. Choose a candle whose smell you love—nothing too strong, but something you truly enjoy sniffing. Light it and then start to slow down your breathing as you enter a mindful meditative state. For most people, it helps to have a darkened room, but if you like to be in the light, that's fine too. You can do this one of two ways. First, you can watch the flame dance and let your mind focus. For some people, a focal point helps them center. The second way to use candles is to close your eyes and simply focus on the scent. Use breathing to center yourself and keep bringing yourself back to calm as your mind wanders. Most people love working with candles because of the pleasant smell. It does take some alone time, though, so it may not work as an everyday practice. However, if you can find some free time, it is a great way to get yourself into a mindful mindset.

CHAPTER 14

What is Holding You Back?

M any people have heard about mindfulness but have not yet engaged in it. Other people have tried it, but upon finding little success they stopped practicing it. It is already evident that mindfulness positively affects the body, the mind and the emotions, so why would people turn away from it? Here are some common reasons and their responses:

"I tried mindfulness but it doesn't fit my schedule."

The bottom line is that everyone is busy these days. Between work, home, hobbies and sleep, no one has an abundance of time anymore. Unless you are completely retired on a good pension or under 10 years old, you probably have a packed schedule. Some people mistakenly believe that mindfulness requires hours of free time. The truth is that it doesn't! This is the beauty of mindfulness—its practice can be squeezed into any setting at any time. Even if you can find only a few moments here and there, you can still reap the benefits of the practice. And, you can squeeze it in during any of your regularly scheduled daily activities. All you have to do is want to be mindful. Once you make that decision, you can learn how to center yourself with the goal of mindfulness in a variety of settings. You can try it when you sit down at the dinner table for a few moments, when you drive to work, when you brush your hair in the morning, when you fold laundry. The point is to do what you normally do, but to do it with a keen mindfulness to the "now" of the experience. If you are folding clothes, feel the heat emanating off them from being in the dryer. If you are driving to work, at a red light make yourself aware of the leather on your steering wheel and the feel of the seat at your back. If you are at the dinner table, pay attention to the smell and taste of the food. Don't just go through the motions; pay close attention to what all your senses are privileged to experience. Draw everything you can from each and every experience you have.

> *"I tried mindfulness but my mind kept wandering so I gave up."*

Even the most spiritually advanced yogi master who meditates and practices mindfulness numerous times a day didn't start out that way. He or she started in the exact place you are. He or she "heard about" mindfulness, but wasn't ready to engage in it. When the yogi master did, he or she most likely went through the same things you did: distraction, having miscellaneous thoughts crop up. Perhaps he or she even thought a few times about throwing in the towel. Here's the difference. First, the yogi had the tools necessary to re-center himself or herself time and again. In addition, the yogi master used those tools time and again. Second, the master was determined to quiet his or her mind of the chatter and get to the "now." Regardless of what happened, the yogi master got back into a mindful mindset and tried to stay there. The interesting thing about the human mind is that, yes, it can process thousands of things per second. However, it can also follow directions. When you decide to be mindful, your mind wants to rush from thought to thought because it is accustomed to doing so; however, it also wants to center on one thought like you want it to do. Because these desires oppose each other, the mind must pick one or the other. As you purposely keep drawing it back to the focus of mindfulness, it will opt for what you want rather than what it wants to do. How long will this take? No one can say. You might see changes after two weeks, you may need two months. The fact is, though, that those changes will occur. You will find that as you practice being mindful, your brain will learn to let go of other things more quickly. It may take time, but it is natural that if you keep training your mind, it will follow.

> *"I would love to be mindful but I don't have free time throughout my day."*

This is tied to the person who thinks that his or her life is just too busy for mindfulness. The reality is that everyone is busy and burdened by various things. Everyone has lives that are moving very quickly. That doesn't mean everyone must forgo the very thing that can help keep them sane. Being mindful isn't an act that takes an hour out of your day, seven days a week. You can easily take any time during which you aren't doing something to slow down and become acutely aware of the world around you. As you engage in a task, think about the senses of taste, smell, touch, hearing and sight. Combine each into your experience. For example, let's say you find yourself in the office's conference room working on a presentation. Feel your fingers on the laptop. Hear the light buzz of the machines in the room. See the lights on the ceiling. If you are rushing to pick up coffee in the morning at your local coffee shop, pay attention to the smells that are abundant in the shop. Focus on the taste of your coffee as you sip it from the cup. Pay attention to how the cup feels in your hand. Being mindful is not an overwhelming act that takes hours of planning. It can easily be worked into your day during your regular activities. Some people like to set a timer on their phone twice a day, once in the late morning and once in the early evening. When the timer goes off, wherever they are, whatever they are doing, these people remember mindfulness and practice it. This is a great way to get your mindful mindset into your day without having to stop and completely alter it.

"I want to be mindful but my family life is too hectic right now."

This is the age-old issue of waiting for the right time to do something. Consider times in your life when you waited for the "right time." It may have happened eventually but you lost a lot of time waiting. With mindfulness, the benefits are abundant—physical, emotional and mental—so losing time before you start to engage in them limits you in many ways. This is why it is important to find small bits of time during which you can incorporate it into your life. There is no reason to put off the very thing that could benefit your entire being. On top of that, if your life is so hectic, this is the perfect time to find mindfulness. It is difficult to manage hundreds of tasks day in and day out, over and over. Without respite, you may feel overly stressed or anxious. You may even want to throw in the towel. When you practice being mindful, you slow all that down, even if only for a few minutes here and there. The very act of slowing things down can ease the hectic nature of your day entirely. This is a tool that can help you manage the stress and hectic nature of your day. One thing you can always do is find time to be mindful as you move throughout your day. Centering your mind will not just benefit you spiritually, it will help you handle all those other hectic things you must tackle throughout your day. How many times have you found yourself on auto-pilot as you rush to get things done? Doing them with mindfulness can completely change your experience of life. It will help you understand what you are doing and find the true value in all your actions.

"Mindfulness is for religious people who want to get closer to God."

Mindfulness is not something that has any label on it like "religion." It is an activity that has been proven to benefit those who practice it on a physical level, a mental level and an emotional level. It has nothing to do with any one religion, or with religion at all. People from all walks of life practice it because they realize the intrinsic value it brings them. Yes, of course, some of them are religious-minded, but a large portion aren't. They merely see the benefits that mindfulness creates. The reason it is so valued in different cultures is because it gives people the ability to be sharper when they are completing their everyday tasks. Their brains grow accustomed to focusing on one thing rather than numerous things. You have likely heard the phrase "Jack of all trades, master of none!" This is used for people who know a little about a lot of things but aren't proficient at any one thing. The same can be applied to thoughts. People who can't center on their thoughts and quell their minds are jumping around without giving themselves the opportunity to become focused on one. With mindfulness, you get that opportunity. By using simple breathing techniques and listening to your body, you can draw out the true value of every experience to which you find yourself privy. This is a way to garner as much value from all your daily activities. Religion is not part of that, nor is any religion to which you may currently tie yourself. The value is for everyone who is able to slip into a true knowing of the "now" and value it as a unique experience. Opening all the senses to let them do what they are supposed to do makes you acutely aware of life on a more in-depth level of true knowing.

"Mindfulness is for spiritual people."

Again, mindfulness is not limited to those who are spiritual in any way. After years of experimentation and study, psychologists have found that mindfulness can help with everything from depression to anxiety to ADHD to chronic arthritis. If it were merely for the spiritual, it would be a spiritual act that affected only spirituality. The reality is that it affects much more than that. Numerous studies have been done in "real-life" situations to see what its efficacy truly is. For example, a school system in California tested mindful studies and practices on its student body. These were students who were formerly part of the lower performing and low-attendance groups. After allowing students to engage in their own mindfulness studies throughout the day, the district noted that attendance was up, and so were grades. The district also had a lowered record of incidents of anger and outbursts. The fact is, mindfulness is useful for much more than merely spiritual growth. It helps the mind function on a more streamlined level. It helps train the brain to organize thoughts better, rather than managing them as they haphazardly come into play. Just think about a day; you likely have thousands of thoughts rushing through your brain—things to do, things to remember. They cloud your mind and rob you of the "now." By learning to quiet them, you can reap the true value of the "now." Rather than continuing to ignore it, for the first time, you will feel it. This practice is not for the spiritual; it is for those who want to make the most of their experiences with life. They want to help their bodies maximize performance on a physical, emotional and mental scale. By using mindfulness, they tap into a tool that helps them positively affect all three at the same time.

"This is for people who aren't as stressed out as I am."

The fact is, mindfulness is for everyone—the more stressed you are, the more likely you need it. One thing you'll find with purposefully being mindful is that you get to slow down and experience life. If your life is hectic, you likely rush through it performing one task after another. There is little time when you're constantly rushing to stop and "smell the proverbial roses." This is why a hectic life is ideal for being mindful. You can ease it into your day and start to truly appreciate the things that are happening within it. Studies have shown that being mindful is a great way to manage stress. The reality is that stress is not good for your body. It can cause problems with the cardiovascular system; it can cause anxiety and depression. Stress is not a good thing, but many people can't avoid it due to their lifestyles. If this is you, consider using it to ease your body's and mind's stress level, if only for a few moments here and there. You can easily start being mindful a few times a day, for a few minutes at a time. You don't have to completely stop what you are doing to take part. As you shower, as you drive, as you pour coffee, as you take the dog out, you can quiet your mind and be aware of the "now." You can then train your mind to settle itself and find that it helps your mind handle some of the other stressors you encounter throughout your day. There are tools that can assist you when you are handling stress. Ignoring it and withstanding it aren't enough. You need proactive tools to help you…and mindful practices are just the thing!

"I'm not into New Age thinking."

New Age thinking was a fad a few decades ago that caught on with a group of believers. It turned into a quasi-religion and is still a strong movement now. It is not, however, the same thing as being mindful. Rather, New Age is a movement that focuses on mysticism, holism and spirituality. It may use mindful practices, but the two are not synonymous. The New Age also incorporates a wide range of extra beliefs and practices. Mindfulness is something that everyone from all walks of life can do. It isn't exclusive to any religion or lifestyle. The benefits are plentiful, and that is why mindfulness is so popular among so many different people. You don't have to be "into" any one religious segment, or be religious at all, to find the true benefits of being mindful. As you start practicing it, you will find that it helps your brain function more efficiently and handle more things with clarity. This is the value it brings that is unique to the practice. If you are accustomed to doing "one thousand things a day," this may be the exact practice you need to reap the true benefits of your day. It allows you to keep seeing the value of every experience through your five senses. Normally we do these things subconsciously, which doesn't make them a true value in our lives. When you slow down and become mindful, you start to see the value. You experience everything before you. Having a few times every day that allow you to see this value and experience life can bring you a new appreciation of your life and what you want. It is important to remember that this is not a New Age practice; it is not a practice specific to any one religion.

CHAPTER 15

Conclusion

Now that you have a general view of what mindfulness is and how it can benefit you, it is time to start using it! Remember that you don't need any special tools to start. It is simply a matter of focusing on the "now" and aligning your mind with its experience of being. Once you get started, you'll start reaping the benefits of total body wellness and improvement.

About the Author

Zoey Matthews has been infinitely passionate about helping people for as long as she can remember. Today, she utilizes that unwavering passion to advocate for children and teach others the art of success. To many, Sylvia is an acclaimed Researcher, Author, and Self-Publisher. However, she sees herself as someone who is simply trying to make a positive impact in people's lives through her multifaceted work.

Thank You

I hope this book was able to help you
to bring yourself back to awareness.

Finally, if you enjoyed this book, then I'd like to ask you for a favor:

Would you be kind enough to leave a review for this book? It'd be greatly appreciated!

Thanks again, and good luck!

67378330R00042

Made in the USA
San Bernardino, CA
22 January 2018